ESSENTIAL QUESTIONS
for
END TIMES

what can we know for sure?

ESSENTIAL QUESTIONS
for
END TIMES

what can we know for sure?

M David McKillen

E: whatintheworldishappening@gmail.com

with

David McGahie & Jonathan Black

RITCHIE

John Ritchie Publishing

ISBN-13: 978 1 914273 28 5

www.ritchiechristianmedia.co.uk

All Bible quotations have been "italicised" with double speech marks.
All other quotations / references within single speech marks.

Titles referring to names of God have been capitalised.
Bible references have been abbreviated – for sake of space – using the first
three letters of a Book title, then the chapter and the verse. e.g.
(1 Samuel chapter 1 verse 10) is written as (1Sam. 1:10).

Old Testament (the mostly Hebrew, BC, section of the Bible) is written as O.T.
New Testament (the mostly Greek, AD, section of the Bible) is written as N.T.

Typeset & Cover Design by Brian Chalmers Design Services:
www.brianchalmersdesign.co.uk
Chart & Images design by Martin Kenny Design & Illustration Services, Belfast.
Copyright Photographs by Unsplash, Montreal, QC ©. Unless otherwise stated.
Printed by Bell & Bain Ltd., Glasgow.

[Eng.UK]

essential **questions:**

what's going to happen **next**?

Global nuclear war … or not? 'Mutually Assured Destruction' – Does anyone know?

Everyone has 'life questions': Some personal, some painful, some fearful. We all have questions because nothing in life seems secure, or stable any longer. Things we thought were 'certainties' have all become shaky. Places where we thought there were boundaries and borders – there are now only gaps and dangers. The road of life has become full of potholes. We shelter within our media-network bubble, until something breaks in and alarms. Our world is full of sirens ...

Many long for contentment, security, safety, and comfort. Yet all these are temporary as well. Moses, one of the early Bible prophets, said, *"The years of our life … are soon gone, and we fly away … So teach us to number our days that we may get a heart of wisdom"* (Psa. 90:10,12).

We need serious answers to serious questions, while there is still time.

Are there answers we can trust?   **Can we know what is truth?**

is **anyone** out there?

'All matter started from a single point, a few millimetres across, before expanding outwards.' This concept, formulated by the American cosmologist Edwin Hubble (1929), became known as the 'Big Bang Theory'. It encompasses not only the origin of all matter, the universe, but also mankind. Coupled with the existing 'Theory of Evolution' which has now been taught in the world of education and science for well over 100 years.

life from non-life?

These 'theories' – which have been generally accepted by many – have deep underlying difficulties. One major question is, 'Where did life come from?' The **law of biogenesis** states: 'Living organisms are produced only by other living organisms'. **All life derives from preceding life**.

The idea that life can come from 'non-life' (abiogenesis) is assumed – only by evolutionists – to have occurred a few times in evolutionary history. Not though as a result of any known scientific evidence, but because the dominant worldview in modern western science (atheism), 'requires a chance spontaneous origin of life'. [1]

more laws of science ...

The law of conservation of energy (the 1st law of thermodynamics) states that energy is neither being created nor destroyed. Matter can be converted into energy, but the sum total of both cannot be changed. Therefore, the universe began by a cause outside of itself. The biblical account of creation agrees; God "*worked*" for six days and on the seventh day He stopped: Literal consecutive "*days*" of "*evening and morning*".

The law of entropy – the degree of disorder in a system – (the 2nd law of thermodynamics) states, 'The entropy of an isolated system always increases'. Entropy is called, in simple terms, 'Time's Arrow'. It always points down! Over time everything in our universe deteriorates, decays, and dies. [2]

NASA/ESA Hubble (Nov 2009) 'Tucana' Constellation – 170,000 Light Years distant!

The 'Big Bang Theory' and 'Evolutionary Theory' both contradict known scientific laws. Galloway and Noble wrote, 'If we 'follow the science' … we still encounter more than a few anomalies. The biggest of these arise from assumptions … that lack a solid evidence base'. [3]

so what?

To 'believe' is a God-given faculty; mankind is more than a 'superior animal'. **But what to believe is crucial:** 'True science points to the concept of a living … 'First Cause'' [4]. The need for the existence of a supernatural beginning outside of the universe is implied by the laws of physics and is clearly stated – without conflict – in the written Scripture record.

However, biblical faith is not 'blind faith'. Nor conjecture altered continually to suit relatively modern theories. The Bible record points to an eternal Creator, pre-existing all that has been created: *"By faith we understand that the universe was created by the Word of God, so that what is seen was not made out of things that are visible."* (Heb. 11:3).

But the greatest question of all is: **'Who made me?'**

[1] Bergman, J. R. cited, *'in six days'* (Green Forest, AR: Master Books 2019) Pgs. 40-41.
[2] Abou-Rahme, F. *'and God said'* (Kilmarnock, UK: John Ritchie Ltd., 2022) Pg. 66.
[3] Galloway, D. & Noble, A. *'Follow the Science?'* (Kilmarnock, UK: John Ritchie Ltd., 2021) Pgs. 32-33.
[4] Walter, J. L. cited, *'in six days'* (Green Forest, AR: Master Book 2019) Pg. 20.

who made me?

The biblical record is definitive: *"In the beginning, God created …"* (Gen. 1:1). Not only the universe, but also mankind: *"The Lord God formed the man of dust from the ground and breathed into his nostrils the breath of life, and the man became a living creature"* (Gen. 2:7).

So, 'spontaneous generation' is not the answer! Here again is the principle that 'life can only come from life.' In the case of mankind – us – it is more than the creation, or formation, of matter. It is God's life 'breathed in' to humanity. **[1]**

'Why should this be hard to believe? We know that all human characteristics are 'spelled out' in our DNA code, about 2 metres long, coiled up when life begins as a tiny ball the size of a dot on this page!' No timeframe – however long – could achieve such complexity. **[2]**

Life can only be the result of creation and not from random chance!

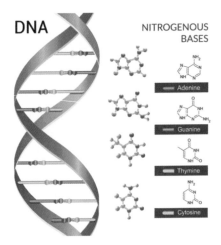

DNA

NITROGENOUS BASES

Adenine

Guanine

Thymine

Cytosine

H. S. Lipson (writing from a neutral perspective) said, 'The only acceptable explanation is creation … we must not reject a theory that we do not like if the experimental evidence supports it.' **[3]**

Once we accept that the 'Genesis record' is scientifically sound – then we must also accept the implications for mankind and his origin …

10

origin by design = purpose?

The biblical record states that God made man in His likeness: *"Then God said, 'Let us make* _man_ *(mankind)* in _our image_, after _our likeness"_ (Gen. 1:26). Mankind is a special – and superior – creation. Unique among all the beings and animals that God made. We are not of the same order as the domestic animal, the farm animal, or the wild beast. We have a *"spirit"* that came from, and connects us to, God. Which cannot be destroyed ...

Mankind was created to be God's representative on earth. With authority over all living creatures (though not the spirit world). God said, *"And let* _them_ *(male and female)* have _dominion_ over the fish of the sea and over the birds of the heavens and over the livestock and over all the earth and over every creeping thing that creeps on the earth"* (Gen. 1:26).

[underlined by author]

a long way down

'But', you say, 'I thought mankind was improving. Did we not come from inferior creatures? Like 'ape-men'?' **No. We did not.** Not only is there no evidence in the biblical record, but there is also no evidence in the scientific record either. Some archaeologists, like Dubois, have confessed later in their lives that what were exhibited as 'missing links' were only invented. Richard Leaky said that some samples of prehistoric species were nothing more than, 'imagination made of plaster of Paris'. [4]

Mankind came directly from the hand of God, perfectly suited to carry out the purposes which He had intended. And to have a permanent relationship with their Creator and superior. Forever.

We must accept that we – the human race – are not in that position today. Nor have we been for a great many generations in the past.

We should ask: **'What went wrong?'**

[1] Abou-Rahme, F. *'and God said'* (Kilmarnock, UK: John Ritchie Ltd., 2022) Pg. 66.
[2] Abou-Rahme, F. *'and God said'* (Kilmarnock, UK: John Ritchie Ltd., 2022) Pg. 67.
[3] Lipson, H. S. *'Physics Bulletin'* (IOP Publishing May 1980) Pg. 138.
[4] Leaky, R. cited, *Weekend Australian* (Sunny Hills, NSW: May 1983) Pg. 3.

what went **wrong**?

All actions have consequences. 'All actions have equal and opposing reactions' (Newton's 3rd law of motion). Even the physical universe is bound by these laws. **God is the original lawgiver.** There cannot be 'law' without a 'lawgiver'. Though we might enact 'laws' today – by democratic vote or by autocratic dictatorship – the universe could not have 'invented' the observed laws by which it operates, and has been maintained: orbits, gravitational force, seasons, etc. [Pgs. 8-9].

order to chaos

We talk of 'Edenic conditions' even if we have no idea what the *"garden in Eden"* looked like. You may imagine the story as a 'Jewish fable', perhaps with a moral meaning, but the Bible records it as very real. How beautiful we cannot imagine. More beautiful and pure than the most 'heavenly' scene on earth today. God put our 'first-parents' in a pristine and pleasant environment. Which we are not in today. **Who can we blame?** The prime polluter of our environment is mankind himself. **Where did it go wrong?** What was the 'external influence' on the order then, to the chaos we see today? Humanity has been destroying our once beautiful planet. **Why?**

enter the serpent ...

Satan [more of him later] was created as a high angel. Possibly the highest. His pride brought him down. His desires – not even his actions – brought judgment by God and his fall (Eze. 28). Exactly when we are not told, but before he appeared in the garden in Eden, and the *"serpent"* – the reptile – allowed Satan to use him to communicate with Eve, the first woman ...

God had said, *"You may surely eat of every tree of the garden, but of the tree of the knowledge of good and evil you shall not eat, for in the day that you eat of it you shall surely die"* (Gen. 2:16-17). Plain enough surely?

But Satan lied directly about the penalty God had set. **He claimed there were no consequences for wrong actions.** The woman was attracted by the outward appeal of the *"fruit"*. She was deceived by the words of the serpent. She took, she ate, she gave to her husband, and he ate too. They knew at once that they had sinned. And hid from God. **How come?**

conscience at work

They had an 'awareness' of their wrongdoing. As do we. But where does that come from? If we 'evolved' from inferior – and inanimate – lifeforms: **How do we know – instinctively – right from wrong?** The man and the woman hid from God because they knew they had disobeyed Him. This was the original sin of man which spread to all of humanity: *"Therefore, just as sin came into the world through one man, and death through sin, and so death spread to all men because all sinned"* (Rom. 5:12).

and God said ...

Over 4,000 times in the Old Testament *"God"* or the *"LORD"* speaks directly. Here God spoke to the serpent, the woman, and the man: Judgment on all. **Deterioration – decay – death**. But also, **deliverance**. The *"offspring"* of the woman would be in conflict with the *"offspring"* of the serpent, but *"He shall bruise your head"* (Gen. 3:15). God would reveal more, as time would pass, and His promises would become clearer ...

The big question is: **'Does God still speak to us today?'**

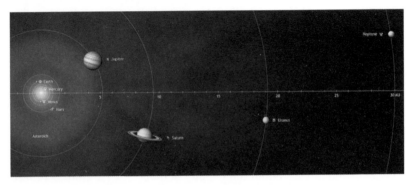

Earth & our sun 150 million kilometres away – our axial tilt 23.5 degrees – our gravitation 9.8 m/s

God speaks in the sky

"The heavens declare the glory of God, and the sky above proclaims His handiwork. Day to day pours out speech, and night to night reveals knowledge" (Psa. 19:1-2). The visible universe – our night sky – does not need a 'translation'. God speaks of His power as Creator in the heavens.

Our earth environment – though polluted – is unique among all planets to sustain vegetative and animal life. We have existed on earth for 1,000s of years because God made it to be so. **And He alone will end it** [Pgs. 52-53]. Yet millions of people, for 1,000s of years, have deliberately ignored God's witness in the heavens!

God speaks in our spirit

René Descartes said, 'I think, therefore I am', but we should ask, 'What do we think about?' We have discussed 'conscience' – the built-in awareness of right and wrong – but we also have a 'God consciousness'. The acknowledgment that a 'Supreme Being' is 'out there' beyond our world.

Why? The Bible has the answer, *"He has made everything beautiful in its time. Also, He has put eternity into man's heart"* (Ecc. 3:11). Our awareness of infinity and immortality. Of an 'afterlife' – after this life – all comes to us from a God-awareness within mankind, put there from the beginning.

God speaks in the scriptures

God has been speaking for over 3,600 years from His written Word. The Bible – as we know it today – has an arrangement of 66 books. Written by over 35 authors. Penned across 1,600 years. Covering – at the end of the O.T. period – 4,000 years in the past and 3,000+ years into the future.

Just men's thoughts? *"No prophecy of Scripture comes from someone's own interpretation … but men spoke from God as they were carried along by the Holy Spirit"* (2Pet. 1:20-21). *"All Scripture is breathed out by God and profitable for teaching … for correction, and for training …"* (2Tim. 3:16).

Many hundreds of prophecies from the Bible have already been fulfilled. Many in relation to the first coming of Jesus. [1]

The Bible gives clear instruction about:
our origin
We are miracles of existence and complexity. We require a Creator. The Bible tells us our Creator is God. He made us and He sustains us.
our purpose
'Man's chief end is to glorify God, and to enjoy Him forever' [2]. **How so?** Mankind was put on earth to represent and to glorify God. But 'enjoying' Him ended at the first rebellion, in Eden's Garden long ago (Gen. 3).
our morality
"The work of the law is written in their (our) *hearts, while their conscience also bears witness, and their conflicting thoughts accuse ... them"* (Rom. 2:15).
Sounds familiar? Outside of God's 'laws' we have no accurate moral guide.
our destiny
We do not create our destiny. But we can choose it. By faith in God's Word. God gave us meaning, and God gave us choice. We are not bound by fatalism. **We can be saved by faith**. *"Therefore, since we have been justified by faith, we have peace with God through our Lord Jesus Christ"* (Rom. 5:1).
Faith in what, or Who?

[1] McKillen, M. D. *'End Times for Beginners'* (Kilmarnock, UK: John Ritchie Ltd., 2021) Pgs. 50-51.
[2] *'Westminster Shorter Catechism'* (1647) Question & Answer No. 1.

one God or many?

God is not a 'thing'

A 'being in the sky' as He is often referred to. Something 'unknown and unknowable'. **God is a Person**. Not – until the birth of Jesus – with a discernible and tangible body, but a real Person with divine character.

The creation record says, *"In the beginning, God created the heavens and the earth"* (Gen. 1:1). This word *"God"* in Hebrew is plural – more than two – indicating the 'Trinity' and unity of God right from the very beginning.

God is not an idol

God forbade the making of any *"carved image"* to represent even Himself (Exo. 20:4). The early history of mankind is characterised by the substitution of the worship of God, on the basis of faith, with the worship of 'gods' that could be seen. Which does not require faith. In the Bible record this idol-worship began in Babylon in Mesopotamia (Gen. 11:1-9).

The early Egyptians had 'over 2,000 deities'; gods to whom they gave 'anthropomorphic forms' for every aspect of life, and after-life. [1]

The ancient Greeks and Romans had 12 'supreme gods' who were supposed to live on Mount Olympus. All these gods were not only represented in idol form, but – in all of these 'manmade' religions – a great continual ritual of appeasement was needed, year on year, to make the worshippers feel more secure.

Many of the 'religions' of our world still operate on the same cycle of fear, guilt, and a desire to appease a 'god' who cannot be satisfied. Even today.

The 'Parthenon' (c.400BC) - temple of Athena on the Acropolis in Athens

God is supreme

Not only **ever existing** but **all knowing**. *"I am God, and there is no other … there is none like Me, declaring the end from the beginning and from ancient time things not yet done"* (Isa. 46:9-10).

God is **all powerful**: He says, *"Behold I am the Lord, the God of all flesh. Is anything too hard for Me?"* (Jer. 32:27). God is above all that is called 'god'. He is the one true God, and He has – **because He is a loving God** – made a way by which we can approach Him. Not based on what we do (or pay), but based on what Jesus Christ, God's Son, has already done [Pgs. 26-29].

God is Spirit

He has been – eternally – and always will be: *"God is spirit, and those who worship Him must worship in spirit and truth"* (Joh. 4:24). The person who said that, to a woman by a well, revealed Himself as *"Messiah"* in a body.

God is Son

The Son was always there, in Spirit: *"In the beginning was the Word … and the Word was God … And the Word became flesh and dwelt among us"* (Joh. 1:1,14). The *"Word"* who *"spoke"* at creation, became 'God in flesh'. Who was born into our world – in a body – more than 2,000 years ago:

Why was it necessary for Jesus to be born?

[1] Mark, J. J. *'Gods of Egypt'* World History Encyclopaedia (2016).

what is **sin**?

Not all major 'world religions' define 'sin' in the same way. For example, 'The idea of sin or original sin has no place in Buddhism' [1]. This is foreign to the teaching of the Bible, and to a thinking that many would agree with! The Oxford English Dictionary defines sin as, 'an immoral act considered to be a transgression against divine law'. The first mention of *"sin"* in the Bible indicates that it is associated with **self-will**, **lack of belief** in what God had said, **rebellion** in the mind and **disobedience** in action (Gen. 4:3-12).

a world with no sin

Consider the environment our 'first-parents' were in: No sin, no shame, no sorrow, and no separation from God. No wonder that we have asked already, **'What went wrong?'** Yet by the time we reach the *"days of Noah"* we find that *"The earth was corrupt in God's sight, and the earth was filled with violence"* (Gen. 6:11). God judged the 'old world' in a global flood; the evidence of which is etched on our sedimentary geology, and told out in ancient history and mythology, world over. **How sobering is that?** [2]

crime and punishment

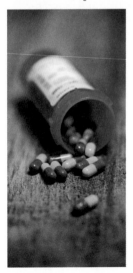

In our world today over 11 million people are in prison. Some will be there because of persecution, yet the country in the world with the highest prison ratio is the U.S.A. (629/100,000) [3]. Even though known as, 'The land of the brave and the home of the free'. The heart of man is the same, world over, there are no exceptions.

Jesus said, *"For from within, out of the heart of man, come evil thoughts, sexual immorality, theft, murder, adultery, coveting, wickedness, deceit, sensuality, envy, slander, pride, foolishness. All these evil things come from within, and they defile a person"* (Mar. 7:21-23).

but I am not a sinner!

How often has that been the response to the biblical accusation, *"All have sinned and fall short of the glory of God"* (Rom. 3:23)? **But wait …**

Have you ever **told a lie?** God's law says, *"You shall not bear false witness".* Have you ever **stolen anything?** God's law says, *"You shall not steal".* Have you **coveted at all?** God's law says, *"You shall not covet … anything that is your neighbour's"* (Exo. 20:13-17).

What about **foolish thoughts?** Do they matter? The Bible says, *"The thought of foolishness is sin"* (Pro. 24:9 KJV).

sin brings a penalty

Every 'cause' must have an 'effect', as we have seen. The effect of sin is shame, a sense of guilt, a separation from God.

Not just in time, but spiritually in the 'after-life' as well. **Forever.**

The Bible says, *"For the wages of sin is death, but the free gift of God is eternal life in Christ Jesus our Lord"* (Rom. 6:23). There will be a final judgment day for all who have refused the *"free gift"* of God, which is forgiveness through the death of His Son, Jesus Christ [Pgs. 28-29; 60-61].

[1] Buddha Dhana Education Association (May 2013).
[2] Whitcomb, J. & Morris, H. *The Genesis Flood* Phillipsburg, NJ: P&R Publishing (1961) Pgs. 123-124.
[3] Institute for Crime & Justice Policy Research (ICPR) Statistics as of Dec. 2021.

is morality absolute?

One question we must face is whether morality – the distinction between what is right and what is wrong – is absolute (defined and fixed) or subjective? Friedrich Nietzsche, a famous philosopher, explicitly denied the existence of God, but accepted that this undermined the reality of morality [1]. Another atheistic philosopher admitted, 'If there are objective (moral) values, they make the existence of a god more probable than it would have been without them' [2]. The problem remains: if something is 'right' or 'wrong' then someone must decide this, and that entity or 'person' must have the authority to do so.

what is the source of morality?

This is a huge problem for those who deny a creator God, believing that we arose from random evolutionary processes [Pgs. 8-9]. How can a universal sense that to murder is wrong 'evolve'? If evolutionary theory is correct, then eliminating individuals which threaten the overall fitness of the species could even be desirable and 'right'. One publication discussing the subject of the 'evolution of morality' – with the intent of defending an evolutionary viewpoint – recognised the obvious difficulty: 'But which behaviours are 'moral'? … One cannot even identify the relevant behaviours without a working concept of 'right' and 'wrong' … Invoking a value judgment threatens to prejudice the whole endeavour.' [3]

God's standards or my preferences?

The Bible clearly presents the creator – *"God"* – as perfect, holy, and just. But also, as loving every human being (Joh. 3:16). As God, He is the very definition of *"good"* (Mat. 19:17). As a loving God, His commandments are what is best for His creation. As a Holy God, He has established an absolute standard from which everyone *"falls short"* (Rom. 3:23). **What is 'right' or 'wrong' has nothing to do with our feelings, preferences, or desires, but has been established by God** [Pgs. 10-11].

can we update our moral code for our times?

The Bible foretold that humankind would seek to do just that! Fundamentally, it comes down to the question, **'Does God establish right and wrong, or do we decide this for ourselves?'** The fact we were created by a Holy God who is the definition of *"good"* means we have no right to change that 'good' to suit our desires, however strong they may be! The Bible predicted that in the last days of this age, the accepted moral standards of society will be far from what God established (2Tim. 3:1-4). God also explains that when society turns  from accepting the truth of their Creator, they will increasingly accept all kinds of sexual sins, and seek satisfaction in ways other than the pattern of heterosexual, lifelong, monogamous, marriage that God had established. Reaping terrible consequences as a result. (Rom. 1:21-32; Mar. 10:6-9).

does God hate non-heterosexual people?

Absolutely not! Quite the contrary. The Bible teaches that God loves the entire world of humanity. However, it places every single one of us in the category *"sinners"* (Rom. 3:23). **Every one of us has character traits that mean we have desires to act in ways which are against the absolute moral standards established by God.** And yet God loves every single person, even if He hates the sin in our lives. The fact that we are born with a natural tendency to desire a certain thing, or to want to behave in a certain way (our freewill), is not proof that the desired behaviour is morally acceptable. It is simply evidence that every one of us belongs to a human race which has fallen and – from Adam – has decayed and degenerated [Pgs. 12-13].

[1] Nietzsche, F., *The Genealogy of Morals* (1887), translated by Horace Barnett Samuel. New York: Courier Dover Publications (2003).
[2] Mackie, J. L. *The Miracle of Theism.* Oxford: Clarendon Press (1982) Pgs. 115-16.
[3] Allchin, D. *The Evolution of Morality.* Evo Edu Outreach 2 (2009) Pgs. 590–601.

made in **God's image?** [D.McG.]

Changing boundaries: It is not only God's moral absolutes that humankind has tried to change throughout history. **Satan seeks to destroy God's glory** by encouraging humanity to challenge and rebel against all boundaries and distinctions established by God in His creation. Right at the start of human history Satan said, *"Did God actually say ...?"* (Gen. 3:1). The theory that mankind gradually evolved from lower animals immediately undermines the difference God made between human beings and the animal kingdom: ***"God created man in His own image ... male and female He created them."*** (Gen. 1:27).

assigned or selected?

This biblical statement, that when creating human beings God assigned them 'binary-gender' (male and female) rather than asking them to decide their 'preference', also goes against modern thinking. There is no denying that some individuals today experience the challenge of gender dysphoria (persistently feeling they are a different gender to their biological sex). There are even concerns that this might be increasingly frequent, partly due to exposure to hormone-disrupting pollutants (endocrine disruptors) in our modern world, although many other factors are involved. [1, 2]

However, the Bible does not describe our 'identity' as something to be achieved or selected, but as something we receive from God.

God first or me first?

As with moral standards [Pgs. 20-21] it is a question of whether we believe that God knows better than us! Years ago, if asked about their identity, most would have responded along the lines of race or ethnic origin. More recently many defined themselves by their career. It has now become common for many to derive their identity from their sexuality. In the Bible, God states that every single human being is made in His image. **This is our principal identity**, even if the *"image"* has become diminished due to mankind's continuing fall from the perfection of that which was there at the beginning [Pgs. 10-11].

do I need another identity?

Being made in God's image brings great dignity! It is the basis for the sanctity of human life. But as sinners we all destroy that dignity regularly. God's offer to save those who accept Jesus Christ as Lord, and make them His children provides the possibility of an even better identity, totally undeserved: *"See what kind of love the Father has given to us, that we should be called children of God"* (1Joh. 3:1). Many people are seeking for an identity. For something to which they can belong.

God offers us the best identity possible

Becoming a Christian will transform our perspective on many issues. Race and skin colour are of no relevance; we are all created in God's image! Male and female equality will not be an issue; both are equally created in God's image! Discrimination based on social status or wealth should never be considered; we are all created equally in God's image! **The need to establish our self-identity in any of those issues should no longer be of primary importance.** Children of the Almighty God are called to live primarily for Him and for His glory.

what if I still have old desires?

Does this mean that if I become a Christian I will never again experience a desire to 'fit in'? Or a sense that I am more like a 'different gender'? Or have 'other attractions'? Or a desire for some other 'identity' of my own choice? Or difficulty with addictions like alcohol, gambling, or drugs? Or other aspects of my past lifestyle? **No, it does not!** Such feelings may linger: We all experience differing temptations throughout our lives. But knowing we were created for a greater purpose, and have a greater identity, will be more important than any 'feelings' we may have. **A desire to please God will become greater than a desire to please ourselves.** In trusting Him, we will know that what He has chosen for us is best. Only a true dependence on God and faith in Jesus Christ can help us. And to those who trust Him, He gives His Holy Spirit to empower them in their new life!

[1] https://www.psychologytoday.com/gb/blog/the-human-beast/201911/gender-fluidity-and-hormone-disruptors
[2] Saleem F, Rizvi S. W. *Transgender Associations and Possible Aetiology*, (December 24, 2017).

can religion help?

According to world statistics 97% of humanity would claim to be 'religious' to some degree. Karl Marx said, 'Religion is the sigh of the oppressed creature ... the soul of soulless conditions. It is the opium of the people'. [1] How hopeless a condition is that?

mankind was made to worship

Since mankind was *"created"* it is biblically logical that we should want to worship our Creator. Jesus summarised all the O.T. law into two statements: *"The Lord our God, the Lord is one. And you shall love the Lord your God with all your heart and with all your soul and with all your mind and with all your strength".* The second follows from the first: *"You shall love your neighbour as yourself"* (Mar. 12:29-31).

love your God – love your neighbour

The problem is so many want to worship a god other than their Creator. And we must admit, we are not very good at loving our neighbour either!

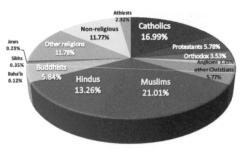

World Religions by percentage (2007 est.)

Main world religions – by percentage – in 2008 [3]

Blaise Pascal said, 'There is a God-shaped vacuum at the deepest level of our being'. [2]

We do have an innate desire – which must be creatorial – to worship 'a god' of sorts.

There are over 4,000 religions and religious bodies in the world today. Some are 'monotheistic' (one god), some 'pantheistic' (many gods), some 'animistic' (animal gods), and some 'atheistic' (no god) which is also a form of religion in itself.

religion says: you must do ...

Christianity says: it is done

There is no greater difference! All religions are humans' attempts to make themselves right with God: By sacrifice, sacrament, services of every sort. But all fall short. God's assessment is, *"All our righteous deeds are like a polluted garment … our iniquities, like the wind, take us away"* (Isa. 64:6).

'New St. Peter's Basilica' (constructed 1506-1615) – St. Peter's Square, Vatican City

why should we travel down the pathway of 'do' if we can never do enough? And never – by our own efforts – come to *"peace with God"*?

True Christianity stands unique (It is not the conglomerate of 'Catholics', 'Protestants', 'Orthodox' and 'Anglicans'). It is those who by faith believe that another has taken their penalty. The *"only begotten Son"* of God *"gave Himself for me"* (Joh. 3:16; Gal. 2:20 KJV).

Paul wrote, *"For by grace you have been saved through faith. <u>And this is not your own doing</u>; it is the gift of God, <u>not a result of works</u>, so that no one can boast"* (Eph. 2:8-9).

[underlining by author]

what is the answer?

The answer is found in the coming into the world of Jesus Christ.

[1] Marx, K. *'Introductions …'* (1843) trans. O'Malley, J. & J. (Oxford, UK: O.U.P. 1970).
[2] Pascal, B. *'Pensées'* (1670) trans. (London, UK: Penguin 1993) Pg. 45.
[3] *TheGreenEditor*, Public Domain, via Wikimedia Commons (2008).

was Jesus just a prophet?

no! Jesus always was - and is - the only Son of God

Paul speaks of, *"the gospel of God, which He promised beforehand through His prophets in the Holy Scriptures, concerning His Son, who was descended from David according to the flesh and was declared to be the Son of God … Jesus Christ our Lord"* (Rom. 1:1-4). Many O.T. prophecies have already been fulfilled at the first coming of Jesus, who was 'the sole individual in history who has matched the prophetic fingerprint of God's anointed'. [1]

God the Son became man

Though prophesied throughout the O.T. – from the first promise in Eden (Gen. 3:15) – it took 1,000s of years for this event to take place. Many prophets were sent with messages from God, some of whom were listened to, and many who were not. Many were martyred for the message they brought, for a prophet from God did not always bring 'good news'.

"Long ago, at many times and in many ways, God spoke to our fathers by the prophets, but in these last days He has spoken to us by His Son, whom He appointed the heir of all things, through whom also He created the world" (Heb. 1:1-2). We have seen that this world, as God created it, had a beautiful environment for pure people. **It was contaminated by Adam's sin. As was mankind as well.** God judged the sin and disobedience. He also promised a remedy, the 'seed of the woman', who one day must come …

because only God could solve the sin problem

God did this by sending His eternal Son, Jesus Christ, to be our Saviour. A divine 'rescue mission' of God to earth to save us from our sins, and from banishment from God for ever. **If Jesus had been 'just a prophet', or even 'a son of god' by birth, then His death would never have been effectual for the guilt of others.** John, the apostle wrote, *"We have seen and testify that the Father has sent His Son to be the Saviour of the world"* (1Joh. 4:14).

[1] Strobel, L. *'The Case for Christ'* (Grand Rapids, MI: Zondervan, 2016) Pg. 202.

fulfilled Messianic prophecies

THE LIFE OF JESUS

PROPHECY		FULFILMENT
"Behold, the virgin shall conceive and bear a son, and shall call His name Immanuel (God with us)" (Isa. 7:14)	BORN OF A VIRGIN	"When His mother Mary had been betrothed (legally pledged) to Joseph, before they came together she was found to be with child from the Holy Spirit" (Mat. 1:18)
"But you, O Bethlehem Ephrathah, who are too little ... among the clans of Judah, from you shall come forth for Me one who is to be ruler in Israel" (Mic. 5:2)	BORN IN BETHLEHEM	"And Joseph also went up from Galilee, from the town of Nazareth, to Judea, to the city of David, which is called Bethlehem ... And while they were there, the time came for her to give birth" (Luk. 2:4-6)
"And the Spirit of the Lord shall rest upon Him, the Spirit of wisdom and understanding" (Isa. 11:2)	THE SPIRIT OF WISDOM	"In the same hour He rejoiced in the Holy Spirit and said, 'I thank You, Father, Lord of heaven and earth" (Luk. 10:21)
"He had done no violence, and there was no deceit in His mouth" (Isa. 53:9)	LIVE A SINLESS LIFE	"He committed no sin, neither was deceit found in His mouth. When He was reviled, He did not revile in return; when He suffered, He did not threaten" (1Pet. 2:22-23)
"Then the eyes of the blind shall be opened, and the ears of the deaf unstopped; then shall the lame man leap like a deer, and the tongue of the mute sing for joy" (Isa. 35:5-6)	HEAL THE SICK	"The blind receive their sight and the lame walk, lepers are cleansed and the deaf hear, and the dead are raised up" (Mat. 11:5)
"The Spirit of the Lord God is upon Me, because the Lord has anointed Me to bring good news to the poor" (Isa. 61:1)	PREACH GOOD NEWS	"And the poor have good news preached to them" (Matt. 11:5)
"Rejoice greatly, O daughter of Zion! ... Behold, your King is coming to you ... humble and mounted on a donkey, on a colt, the foal of a donkey" (Zec. 9:9)	ENTER JERUSALEM IN TRIUMPH	"And they brought the colt to Jesus and threw their cloaks on it, and He sat on it ... And He entered Jerusalem" (Mar. 11:7,11)

JESUS' DEATH AND RESURRECTION

PROPHECY		FULFILMENT
"Even My close friend ... who ate My bread, has lifted up his heel against Me" (Psa. 41:9)	BETRAYED BY A FRIEND	"But the Scripture will be fulfilled, 'He who ate My bread has lifted up his heel against Me" (Joh. 13:18)
"And they weighed out as my wages thirty pieces of silver. Then the Lord said to me, 'Throw it to the potter'" (Zec. 11:12-13)	SOLD FOR THIRTY PIECES OF SILVER	"Then when Judas, His betrayer, saw that Jesus was condemned, he changed his mind and brought back the thirty pieces of silver ... saying, 'I have sinned by betraying innocent blood ... So they took counsel and bought with them the potter's field" (Mat. 27:3-4,7)
"He was oppressed, and He was afflicted, yet He opened not His mouth; like a lamb that is lead to the slaughter" (Isa. 53:7)	SILENT WHEN ACCUSED	"And Pilate again asked Him, 'Have you no answer to make? See how many charges they bring against you'. But Jesus made no further answer" (Mar. 15:4-5)
"I gave My back to those who strike, and My cheeks to those who pull out the beard; I hid not My face from disgrace and spitting" (Isa. 50:6)	BEATEN AND SPAT UPON	"Then Pilate took Jesus and flogged Him ... They came up to Him, saying, 'Hail, King of the Jews!' and struck Him with their hands" (Joh. 19:1,3)
"He poured out His soul to death and was numbered with the transgressors" (Isa. 53:12)	CRUCIFIED WITH SINNERS	"And with Him they crucified two robbers, one on His right and one on His left" (Mar. 15:27)
"When they look on Me, on Him whom they have pierced, they shall mourn for Him" (Zec. 12:10)	LOOKED UPON AS PIERCED	"But one of the soldiers pierced His side with a spear, and at once there came out blood and water. He who saw it has borne witness" (Joh. 19:34-35)
"And they made His grave with the wicked and with a rich man in His death" (Isa. 53:9)	BURIED WITH THE RICH	"When it was evening, there came a rich man from Arimathea, named Joseph ... And Joseph took the body ... and laid it in his own new tomb" (Mat. 27:57,59-60)
"For You will not abandon My soul to Sheol, nor let Your Holy One see corruption" (Psa. 16:10)	RAISED FROM THE DEAD	"He is not here, for He has risen, as He said. Come, see the place where He lay" (Mat. 28:6)

is the cross the **answer**?

Crucifixion dates from long before Roman times. Early records show that the Persians (c.500BC) practised it for slaves and violent criminals, right through to Roman times, until abolished by Constantine (c.320AD).

It was a thing of horror and a curse!

A *"cross"* could be either an upright 'stake' or two pieces with a 'cross-beam'. The Scripture says, *"Cursed is everyone who is hanged on a tree"* (Gal. 3:13), quoting from the book of Deuteronomy (Deu. 21:22). The O.T. *"curse"* is applied to the death of Jesus, yet it was written by Moses over 1,600 years before Jesus' death took place.

why is the cross important?

Almost one third (33%) of the population of our world claim some association with the sign of the *"cross".* Many see it as having value as a 'symbol', a 'charm' even, a protection against evil. **This is wrong.** The *"cross of Jesus"* (Joh. 19:25) had – and has – significance only as the place, and manner, in which He would die. If we see the *"cross"* as anything more than that, it becomes an idol in itself: something which we have already seen that God has forbidden! [Pgs.16-17]

Whether it was an upright stake (Latin *'stauros'*), or a crossbeam (*'patibulum'*), the *"cross"* in the Scripture record has significance only because of the one who was crucified on it. Peter – another eyewitness of the sufferings of Jesus – wrote, *"He Himself bore our sins in His body on* the tree, that we might die to sin and live to righteousness. By His wounds you have been healed" (1Pet. 2:24). **No sinful man could do that!**

the one who was crucified must be God

We cannot escape that reality. A martyr may die for a cause he believes in, even for a just cause. But no human martyr can make *"atonement"* (a covering over in God's sight) for the sins of others. Bishop Handley G. C. Moule said, 'A Saviour not quite divine, is a bridge broken at the further end' [1]. How graphic, and how true!

God's law demanded a penalty. But God's love provided a substitute: *"But God shows His love for us in that while we were still sinners, Christ died for us"* (Rom. 5:8). Faith alone in Jesus Christ can save us.

did the death of Jesus Christ satisfy God?

The Scriptures prove Jesus was God. Jesus' death proved God's love. His resurrection from the grave proved God's power, and God's satisfaction: *"He* (Jesus) *presented Himself alive to them after His suffering by many* (infallible) *proofs, appearing to them during forty days"* (Act. 1:3).

A 'rock-cut tomb' in Israel – a cave with a stone which rolled across (Mar. 16:1-3)

[1] Moule, H. C. G. 'Christ is All: Sermons from N.T. Texts'. E. P. Ditton & Co. New York, NY (1892).

is the Bible record **true**?

Yes, it must be true …
And a true witness demands a personal response:
The Bible contains prophecy that has already been fulfilled.
The Bible contains proof of the resurrection of Jesus.
The Bible contains evidence of the power of God's love.

The original writings ('*autographs*') that were written down as the prophets spoke, or as God dictated, are long gone. Yet the level of consistency across all copies of all N.T. (Greek) documents is 99.5%. This is across a 'manuscript base' of over 24,000 items and fragments!

the dead sea scrolls

There are 15,000 pieces of O.T. and N.T. documents from the collections found in the Qumran Caves (1946-1956) in Jordan. The oldest complete scroll is a copy of Isaiah (at least 1,000 years older than the previous oldest copy). The earliest piece of a N.T. writing is a 'fragment' of Mark's gospel (7Q5) dated 50AD, followed by pieces of Matthew's gospel (P64,67) dated 66AD, and John (P52) dated 110AD. Each of these writings – even if not originals – date these Gospel records within, or immediately after, the lifetime of their writer.

the Bible beyond compare

There are up to 5,000 early copies of a complete N.T. dating back to 200AD, only 100 years after some of the events contained within. By comparison, the writings of Pliny the Younger (61-113AD) have less than 10 copies, dating from around 800AD. The writings of Tacitus (56-120AD) have around 20 early copies dating from 1100AD. The difference is marked! This puts a huge weight of authenticity on the Gospels' record. Not least the record of the resurrection of Jesus, which is recorded in all four Gospels.

the resurrection - beyond belief?

The reliability of the Gospel records is confirmed – even at a human level – by four key questions, as set out by homicide detective Jim W. Wallace in his best-selling analysis '*Cold-Case Christianity*':

> # **Were the 'eyewitnesses' present**, as they claimed?
> # **Were their 'testimonies' corroborated?** Do they agree?
> # **Were their 'accounts' accurate?** But not 'rote' or 'rehearsed'?
> # **Were they biased?** Could they have had ulterior motives? [1]

Apart from the three 'eyewitness' Gospel writers (Mark, Matthew, and John), the death and resurrection of Jesus is also referred to by other N.T. writers. Peter did not write a 'Gospel' (he may have very likely been involved in Mark's), but he preached the gospel publicly, as recorded by the Gentile doctor Luke, *"Men of Israel, hear these words: Jesus of Nazareth – this Jesus, delivered up according to the definite plan and foreknowledge of God, you crucified and killed by the hands of lawless men. God raised Him up, loosing the pangs of death"* (Act. 2:22-24).

Paul heard the testimony of the 'eyewitness' Stephen, the first Christian martyr (Act. 7:2-51). He was accosted miraculously by Jesus on the way to Damascus, and he later wrote, *"Christ died for our sins in accordance with the Scriptures … He was buried … He was raised on the third day in accordance with the Scriptures … Then He appeared to more than 500 brothers at the one time, most of whom are still alive"* (1Cor. 15:3-6).

the evidence demands a response!

Most of the early N.T. eyewitnesses died for their testimony. That is a position foreign to many. We live in a cynical world. 'What's in it for me?' is a question common in our day. **The answer of the gospel is: Everything**.

Pilate – the Roman judge in Judea – said, *"What shall I do with Jesus …?"* (Mat. 27:22).   **Your answer determines your destiny. Forever**.

[1] Wallace, J. W. '*Cold-Case Christianity*' (Colorado Springs, CO: David C. Cook, 2013) Pgs. 160-252.

does our world have a **future**?

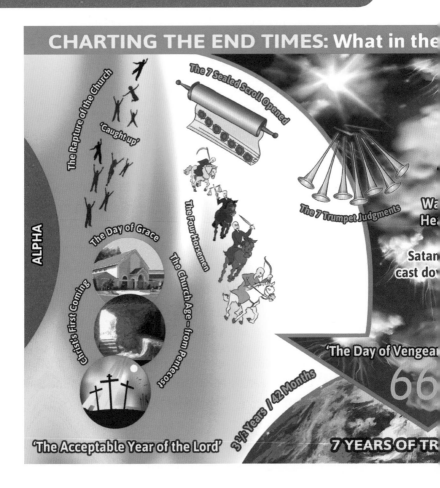

CHARTING THE END TIMES: What in the

ALPHA

The Rapture of the Church

'Caught up'

The 7 Sealed Scroll Opened

The Day of Grace

Christ's First Coming

The Four Horsemen

The Church Age – from Pentecost

The 7 Trumpet Judgments

Wa
Hea

Satan
cast do

'The Day of Vengea

66

'The Acceptable Year of the Lord'   3½ Years / 42 Months   7 YEARS OF TR

is humanity doomed? Most generations of mankind have seen a major crisis of one sort or another. Not all of them global. Some quite local, yet most vicious and horrific for all who have been affected by them.

The 'big questions' in the minds of many – across the world – today are: 'Will there be a WW3?' 'Will humanity be wiped out?' 'Is this the end?' And many other similar fears ...

does mankind have any chance of survival?

is Happening? (Rev. 4 - 22)

The New Jerusalem

The Great White Throne

The 7 Bowl Judgments

The Judgment of the Dead

Christ's Second Coming 'King of Kings'

NEW HEAVEN AND NEW EARTH

OMEGA

The Millennial Kingdom - 1,000 Years

The Fall of Babylon

The Year of My Redeemed

3½ Years / 1,260 Days

Satan Bound 1,000 Years

The Abyss

Lake of Fire – Forever

An original 'End Times' graphic, illustrating the judgments & blessings of God which are future **[1]**

We are going to find out – once again – that the Bible, because it is God's inspired Word, has the answer to these questions and fears. And many more beside. **God has a programme** which has been fixed from before the world began, and cannot be altered. Paul wrote, *"We impart a secret and hidden wisdom of God, which God decreed before the ages for our glory"* (1Cor. 2:7). But as we look into the future we might ask:

what can we know for sure?

[1] McKillen, M. D. *'End Times for Beginners'* (Kilmarnock, UK: John Ritchie Ltd., 2021) Pg. 29.

That depends very much on the vantage point! When a *"prophet"* spoke (and what he spoke about), was also related to the 'when' of the fulfilment of his prophecies. A 'short' prophecy – coming true in the lifetime of the prophet and his hearers – would authenticate 'long' prophecies which might not even be fulfilled (as yet) in our present times. [1]

Jesus prophesied His death. He also prophesied His resurrection. And the time in between: *"We are going up to Jerusalem, and the Son of Man will be delivered over to the chief priests and the scribes, and they will condemn Him to death and deliver Him over to the Gentiles. And they will mock Him and spit on Him, and flog Him and kill Him. And after three days He will rise"* (Mar. 10:33-34). To His followers – back then – these statements were so astonishing that they did not mentally process them. They believed in Jesus as, *"the one to redeem Israel"* (Luk. 24:21). They could not conceive that the greater purpose of God was not only Jesus' death, but His glory!

Jesus prophesied His going away
He said He would leave His disciples for a *"little while"* and then return, speaking of His resurrection which we have examined already [Pgs. 28-29]. He also told of His going back to heaven, to prepare a place for those who believe in Him. He said, *"I am the way, and the truth, and the life. No one comes to the Father except through Me"* (Joh. 14:6).

Jesus also prophesied His coming back
"And if I go and prepare a place for you, I will come again and will take you to Myself, that where I am you may be also" (Joh. 14:3). Jesus is not here – visibly – in a human body, as He was 2,000 years ago. But He will come back, to this earth, in the same body in which He was seen after His resurrection by the first *"witnesses"* to whom He showed Himself alive.

Jesus must return because He said He would ...

What is Jesus doing now?

Two important activities – both of which He foretold He would do – **building His Church** (Mat. 16:18) and **preparing a place for her**. Those were 'long prophecies' when Jesus gave them to His disciples. But they are linked with 'short prophecies' which authenticate them: A very major biblical link.

An "upper room" in a street house in Jerusalem (though not 1ˢᵗ Century AD)

the Holy Spirit sent down

Jesus also prophesied the coming of *"another Helper ... the Spirit of truth"* (Joh. 14:16-17). He would be with the disciples and be in them. The *"Holy Spirit"* – who would not be visible – would be here in the world instead of Jesus being present visibly. **When did this happen?** At *"the day of Pentecost"* (Act. 2:1). This was the 'birth of the Church', which Jesus had prophesied earlier to His disciples, *"I will build My Church"* (Mat. 16:18).

the 'church age'

This is not quite a Biblical description. Jesus defined the time we are living in as, *"the acceptable year of the Lord"* (Luk. 4:19; Isa. 61:2 KJV). He did not say how long it would last, and it has now continued for almost 2,000 years! But the prophet Isaiah foretold that it would be followed by, *"the day of vengeance of our God"* (Isa. 61:2). **A major change is coming soon!**

[1] McKillen, M. D. *'End Times for Beginners'* (Kilmarnock UK: John Ritchie Ltd., 2021) Pgs. 45-46.

will Christians really **disappear**?

If Jesus is coming back – as He promised – for everyone who has believed in Him, then that must include all the Christians since the beginning of the 'Church Age'. John Walvoord said, 'The doctrine of the coming of the Lord for His own, with its promise of the resurrection of the *"dead in Christ"*, and the translation of the living church was a prominent feature in the Church of the first century. Most scholars agree that the early Church … considered it a possibility that the Lord Jesus could come at any time'. **[1]**

is this the 'rapture' teaching?

yes, it is!

At which point someone will say, 'The 'rapture' is an invention. It isn't in the Bible'. The answer to that is twofold; as a doctrine it very clearly is in the Bible. As to the term '*rapture*', it is the word in the Latin Bible which is translated as *"caught up"* in our English Bible (1The. 4:17). **[2]**

Imagine the impact on our world today if – without warning – in every time zone, millions of all the truly *"born again"* believers disappear! Such an event will rock the world from east to west, yet for many it will be the event they have been expecting. Especially as global trends which Jesus predicted – war, earthquakes, famines – are now increasing (Mar. 13:7-8).

what happens next?

Firstly, Jesus **returns** to the air. Secondly, the dead Christians are **raised**, the *"fallen asleep"*. Thirdly, the living believers will be **removed**, they will be *"caught up"*. Fourthly, there will be a **reunion** with each other, and with *"the Lord in the air"*. So that *"hope"* **reassures** us, especially in end times: This is the truth of the '**rapture** of the Church' as summarised by Paul in his letters to the church in Thessaloniki in the 1st Century (1The. 4:13-18). [3]

and after that?

After the removal of the Church comes the *"Tribulation"* [more of that later]. This is a period of increasing turmoil and upheaval. Political unrest, collapse of governments, and realignment of nations. The dominion of a 'global superman' (though he will not rule the whole world), and a specific period which prophecy refers to as *"the time of Jacob's trouble"* (Jer. 30:7 KJV), a period when – once again – the Jewish people will be persecuted. This period is marked by increasing disasters, though all under the control of God, before Jesus comes back, this time to the earth. To set up His kingdom, as a majority of the O.T. prophets promised that He would.

God's resistance now ...

Donald Barnhouse wrote, 'Well, what is keeping *"the Antichrist"* (one of the Bible titles for the devil's superman) from putting in his appearance on the world stage? You are ... and every other (living) member of the body of Christ on earth'. [4]

The Holy Spirit, indwelling each Christian, is part of God's resistance. Paul wrote that, after the Church believers have gone, *"then the lawless one will be revealed, whom the Lord Jesus will kill with the breath of His mouth"* (2The. 2:8). Jesus is not only coming back to *"receive"* us – as we have seen – He is coming to *"deliver us from the wrath to come"* (1The. 1:10).

[1] Walvoord, J. F. *'The Church in Prophecy'* (Grand Rapids, MI: Kregel, 1964) Pg. 111.
[2] McKillen, M. D. *'End Times for Beginners'* (Kilmarnock, UK: John Ritchie Ltd., 2021) Pg. 78.
[3] Hitchcock, M. *'101 Answers About the End Times'* (New York, NY: Multnomah, 2001) Pgs. 80-82.
[4] Barnhouse, D. G. *'Thessalonians Commentary'* (Grand Rapids, MI: Zondervan, 1977) Pg. 99.

Of the present global population, approximately 2.6 billion (33%) are under 20 years old. This has been referred to as, '**the terminal generation**'. What does that mean? Will the adults of tomorrow destroy the world? Will our leaders of today destroy it for our youth?

No. In Bible terms it refers to the possibility that the youth of today will be the generation which Jesus said, *"will not pass away until all has taken place"* (Luk. 21:32). And Jesus said there would be warnings, *"signs of the age"* (Mat. 16:3), so that people – in a day future from when He spoke – would know that the 'end times' were approaching.

Is it possible that this is the generation of today?

is Jesus coming back?

Jesus' disciples wanted to know about end times, just as we do. But they also wanted to know about *"the sign of Your coming and of the end of the age"* (Mat. 24:3). They also wanted to know when Jesus would return!

How many of you – who have read up to here in this booklet – have given any thought to the reality of Jesus coming back?

Jesus spoke of a variety of *"signs"* which would not only be fulfilled, but they would also increase and 'coalesce'. They would come together in increasing frequency, like the *"birth pains"* of an expectant mother. When they begin, they must grow in intensity until the end is accomplished.

what comes at the end?

Then comes the last and greatest sign – after the judgment 'signs' – *"Then will appear in heaven the sign of the Son of Man"* (Mat. 24:30) and at that moment, as promised, Jesus will return. Then the *"King of kings"* will restore our planet, bring peace and justice, and set up a kingdom of righteousness, which will last for 1,000 years (Rev. 20:1-6) [Pgs. 52-53].

Are you ready and waiting for the return of Jesus Christ as the Saviour?

signs of the times?

The "fig-tree" generation: Israel became a Nation again in May 1948. The *"generation (which) will not pass away until all these things take place"* (Mat. 24:34) is the generation which sees Israel as a nation in the land. [1]

"You will hear of wars and rumours" (Mat. 24:6): We live in a day – not just of war – but of 'hearing' and rumour. 'Fake news' is now a tool of war! From 1914 – 1946 almost 160,000,000 died from war, famine, and disease.

"There will be great earthquakes … famines and pestilences" (Luk. 21:11). Today 860,000,000 are officially 'underfed': 10% of our world population. The 'Sars-Cov-2' pandemic had (as of June 2022) 540,000,000 cases within 2.5 years of its identification in the west. And 6.3 million deaths. There are on average 28 earthquakes a day (measuring over 4.5 on the Richter Scale). The total count is many more, and increasing. The U.S.G.S. states that 'severe earthquakes cannot be predicted'. [2]

Is our world out of control? Amir Tsarfati (himself an Israeli born Jew) says, 'When we read the Bible, we can see that God has told us what is to come … God knows what He is doing … **God is in control** … We should not be afraid; we should be encouraged.' [3]

[1] Tsarfati, A. *'The Day Approaching'* (Eugene, OR: Harvest House, 2020) Pgs. 35-40.
[2] United States Geological Survey: www.earthquake.usgs.gov
[3] Tsarfati, A. *'The Day Approaching'* (Eugene, OR: Harvest House, 2020) Pg. 126.

will there be 'WW3'?

Yes! But world events move very quickly. By the time you read this, **WW3** could be history, and **WW4** may be on the horizon! That is only conjecture, based on trends in our world today. But when we look in the Bible – God's Word – we can see that there are 3 or even 4 'world wars' which are still future. Some of them incredibly terrible in their destruction.

A war that will involve all the remaining enemies of Israel (the opponents to a peace treaty of the future) which will have a massive death toll, so that it will take 7 months to remove and bury the corpses (Eze. 39:12).
The war of the 'Seal Judgments' [more on that later] will result in 25% of the global population being slain by warfare and disease (Rev. 6:8).

The *'Battle of Armageddon'* [more on that later] will result in 100% losses by the world armies involved, when Jesus returns (Rev. 16:16; 19:17-21). The 'last battle' – which is not really a battle – will again be against Jerusalem and the Nation of Israel. Once again God will fight on their side, and the death toll of the rebels will be 100% (Rev. 20:9-10) [Pgs. 50-51].

There is a trend here! *"Jehovah"* ('*YHVH*') will do as He has promised. Mark Hitchcock says, 'The Bible is clear that Jesus is coming back again. Make no mistake, He is coming back just as He promised!' **[1]**

but what about nuclear war?

What about 'Mutually Assured Destruction' (M.A.D.): Should we worry? **Can we wipe out our own planet, and ourselves from off its surface?**

No! If we accept the evidence of prophecy, and all the future events that are still to be fulfilled, including the Kingdom of Jesus Christ which will last for 1,000 years on this earth, then we must have confidence, true *"hope"* in the Bible sense of the word. Men cannot go outside the bounds of what God will allow. Even in the worst of human circumstances!

but we have the capability …

Of that there is no doubt. Though nuclear 'warheads' have reduced from the peak of 70,000+ (in 1986) to around 13,000 today, there are still over 7,000 'I.C.B.M.' warheads in storage – some ready and targeted – capable of flying up to 15,000km. One slip, one insane moment could trigger … **But:**

God is in control. This is an increasing theme as we move towards the latter part of our booklet. Neither man, nor devil, is in charge. **Jesus Christ is!**

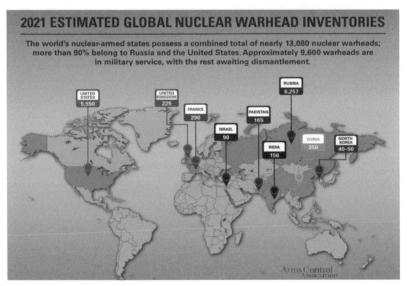

Nuclear warhead distribution map by 'Arms Control Association' (at Jan. 2022) **[2]**

[1] Hitchcock, M. *'101 Answers About End Times'* (New York, NY: Multomah, 2001) Pgs. 200-201.
[2] *'Arms Control Association'* (Washington, DC: 2022): www.armscontrol.org

will there be a **world-ruler**?

Do we have common global problems? Is there a desire for 'central-control'? More importantly, does Bible prophecy predict such things? **Yes!**

'Gasoline prices up 80% in 12 months. Retail goods to rise 50% in 6 months. Fertiliser prices up 300% in 18 months. Milk prices to increase by 50% … Worst winter wheat harvest in recorded history.' **A world out of control?**

Scarcity inflation is now driving the global economy. And may continue to do so. Rob Kapito (of BlackRock Inc.) has said, 'This millennial generation is going to go into a store and not be able to get what they want … a very entitled generation (in the west) that has never had to sacrifice'. [1]

a global 'superman'?

Globalisation has left the western world (and much of the rest) open for the restriction of commodities that individual nations can no longer supply. And the subsequent rise of 'protectionism' following on from such scarcity. **Global problems demand global solutions**. Professor Klaus Schwab says, 'We are at a turning point of humankind, we should not underestimate the historical significance of the state we are in … To improve the state of the world the W.E.F.* is starting the 'Great Reset Initiative''. [2]

These agenda by the World Economic Forum are intended to culminate in the goal of a supreme figure, 'one man to coordinate all', across the boundaries of statehood and sovereignty …   **One man to rule all.**

---

* *World Economic Forum, Geneva, Switzerland*

is this in the Bible?

Yes! Massively so. Mark Hitchcock says, 'Other than Jesus Christ, the (next) most important figure in Bible prophecy – and all of human history – is the coming world ruler; the man called *"Antichrist"* (1Joh. 2:18)'. [3]
More than 100 O.T. and N.T. prophecies describe his character, his career, and his conclusion! He is called, *"a king of bold face"* (Dan. 8:23), *"the prince who is to come"* (Dan. 9:26), *"the one who makes desolate"* (Dan. 9:27), *"the man of sin"* (2The. 2:3 KJV), *"the beast"* (Rev. 11:7; 13:1; 19:20).

who is he?

The Bible supplies significant detail about this coming imposter. He will rise out of southern (or eastern) Europe, part of the ancient Roman Empire. [4]
He will appear with big solutions to many global problems, but he will be a false 'peace-maker'. An agent of Satan. John writes, *"The dragon had given his authority to the Beast"* (Rev. 13:4). He will broker a *"covenant"* with Israel and her neighbours, for 7 years. But he himself will break its terms and support anti-Semitic persecution from the midpoint (Dan. 9:27) [Pgs. 54-55].

does he control all nations?

No! Only Jesus Christ, the *"King of kings"*, in His kingdom will do that.
What about Russia? Whether *"Rosh"* (Eze. 38:2, in some translations) is the Russia of today is open to debate. Whether the *"leopard / tiger"* (Dan. 7:6) is China is also open to question. But the *"hordes … from the uttermost parts of the north … and many peoples with you"* (Eze. 38:6,15) must include Russia. And the *"kings of the sunrising"* (Rev. 16:12 NRB) must, in prophecy, include China. Two of the dominant powers of our world, still evident in the last days. And not dominated by this coming 'global prince'.
What of the U.S.A.? Though much could be speculated upon, one of the great mysteries of future events is this: Does the Bible identify a last days 'super-power' in the west?   **Sadly, that does not seem to be the case!**

[1] Kapito, R. www.blackrock.com (London, UK: Mar 2020).
[2] Schwab, K., Prof. *'The Great Reset'* www.weforum.org (Sept. 2020).
[3] Hitchcock, M. *'101 Answers About End Times'* (New York, NY: Multomah, 2001) Pg. 117.
[4] McKillen, M. D. *'End Times for Beginners'* (Kilmarnock, UK: John Ritchie Ltd., 2021) Pgs. 134-135.

is prophecy **literal**?

One of 11 gates to 'Temple Mount – where the "Abomination" will someday be erected

as it was: so it will be

Solomon the wise king said, *"What has been is what will be, and what has been done is what will be done"* (Ecc. 1:9). When we look back, we see in history 'shadows' of things that still must come. Every prophecy in Scripture that has been fulfilled, up to now, has been done so in exact detail. And every prophecy that has not yet been fulfilled must also happen in detail. The question is: **How literal is future prophecy?**

Dr. D. L. Cooper said, 'When the plain sense of Scripture makes sense, seek no other sense'. Time has proved that even strange prophecies were literal at the point of fulfilment. [1]

What God has determined, He must bring to pass.

Things that have not yet happened – geopolitical events and catastrophes, as well as the direct judgments of God against human wickedness – will not be accidental when they do take place.

God's intervention in the past ages – recorded in Scripture – confirms it. Not only that, but – as Thomas Campbell the Scottish poet wrote – 'Coming events cast their shadows before'. God is giving us a series of warnings of what is about to happen in our world in the last days [Pgs. 38-39].

does the past prove the future?

Jesus foretold the signs of the *"end of the age"* (Mat. 24:3) as we have seen [Pgs. 34-35]. These were 'long prophecies' or *"signs"* which, after 1,900 years, are only being fulfilled now. As we have also seen, a true prophet mixed 'long signs' with 'short signs'; those which would be fulfilled in the lifetime of the generation who heard the prophecies.

At the same time – in His 'Olivet Discourse' – Jesus foretold the destruction of Herod's Temple in Jerusalem: *"Do you see these great buildings? There will not be left here one stone upon another that will not be thrown down"* (Mar. 13:2). This must have seemed incredible – though the King of Babylon had done the same before (606BC). Yet in 70AD, less than 40 years later, Titus the Roman general besieged the city of Jerusalem and destroyed the Temple. To this day the Jews have no Temple, and they have a national day of mourning – *'Tisha ba-Av'* – for that reason on that date.

back to the future

Those who destroyed *"the city and the sanctuary"* (Dan. 9:26) in 70AD, were also predicted in prophecy (c.540BC) to be of the ethnicity of the *"Prince who is to come".* Another O.T. name for the future world leader, soon to appear. Who is also called, as his final title, *"the Beast"* (Rev. 19:20; 20:10). The first part of Daniel's 490-year time-line prophecy was fulfilled in 32AD. The second part (the last 7 years) has not been fulfilled yet. **But it must!**
He will not destroy the *"sanctuary"* in that future day. He will pollute it with an *"image"* and his *"false prophet"* will demand worship of his statue by all (Rev. 13:15). Just as Nebuchadnezzar the King of Babylon did back in Daniel's time (Dan. 3:4). And at the very midpoint of the *"covenant"* period.

The *"Prince"* and the *"False prophet"* are very literal people. The *"beast"* and *"the great red dragon"* may be descriptive terms (Rev. 12:3 and 13:1), but the *"devil and Satan"* (Rev. 20:2) are not: **Satan is a real being**. And, as a part of God's judgments, he and his demons are about to be given increased freedom against humanity, along with his coming human agents.

[1] Cooper, D.L. Dr., (1886-1965) *Bible Research Society* (Los Angeles, CA) www.biblicalresearch.info

is Revelation just a book of symbols?

CHARTING THE END TIMES: What in the World is Happening? (Rev. 4 - 22)

No! The last book of the Bible contains many symbols, possibly because some of the things that the Apostle John saw in vision (in the 1st Century) could not be understood literally. But many things in the book are literal, and – as we have seen – things which appeared 'symbolical' at the time of prophesying, have turned out to be much more 'literal' when fulfilled.

The book of Revelation covers 3 main time periods:
1. *"The acceptable year of the Lord"* (Isa. 61:2; Luk. 4:19 KJV).
2. *"The day of vengeance of our God"* (Isa. 61:2).
3. *"The year of My redeemed"* (Isa. 63:4 KJV) [Pgs. 52-53].

While the Church is still on earth, and before God's final judgment period commences, we are still in stage one. Which some call the '**Church age**'. Jesus made it clear that – though two *'periods'* were in one verse (in Isaiah's prophecy) – there was a 'gap' in the prophecy. The *"acceptable year of the Lord"* (which we are in) would be longer than O.T. prophets imagined. [1]

what is 'the tribulation'?

Though the second period is often called 'the tribulation', and though there will be trouble of every kind [as we have seen], the *"great tribulation"* that Jesus spoke of (Mat. 24:21) applies to the second half. What Jeremiah called in his O.T. prophecy, *"the time of Jacob's trouble"* (Jer. 30:7 KJV).

The third period in the book of Revelation is called the '**Kingdom age**'. We will see at the end of the book that it lasts, on earth, for 1,000 years. [2]

what do the symbols mean?

A great many of the 'symbols' in Revelation are inside the mid-section, the 'judgment period'. Which overall is seven years long. We know this because the 2nd half is referred to as *"42 months"* (Rev. 11:2; 13:5), and the first half as *"1,260 days"* (Rev. 11:3). This seven-year period most likely lines up with the '7 years' outstanding from Daniel's 490-year prophetic 'timeline' (Dan. 9:24-27) foretold to him in c.540BC. [3]

the 7 'seal' judgments

The judgments of God, in the centre section of Revelation (Chps. 6-19), are controlled by the opening of a *"scroll … sealed with seven seals"* (Rev. 5:1). The one who opens them is Jesus Christ. The one who preached *"the acceptable year of the Lord"* will then have His time of judgment. The *"seals"* introduce the 'four horsemen' (possibly one of the best-known symbols), who represent the war, famine, and death that we have already considered [Pgs. 38-39].

the 7 'trumpet' judgments

The trumpet judgments – sounded by angels – are controlled by Jesus Christ also. The judgments intensify, and affect the surface of the earth, and the oceans (Rev. 8-9).

the 7 'bowl' judgments

The bowl judgments come at the very end of the 7-year period, and are the most intense. They are targeted at the *"Beast"*, his kingdom, and all who have taken his identifying *"mark"*. They lead up to *"Armageddon"* [Pgs. 50-51].

The imagery may be symbolic; the judgments are terribly literal!

[1] McKillen, M. D. *'End Times for Beginners'* (Kilmarnock, UK: John Ritchie Ltd., 2021) Pg. 60.
[2] Hitchcock, M. *'101 Answers About the End Times'* (New York, NY: Multnomah, 2001) Pgs. 162-163.
[3] McKillen, M. D. *'End Times for Beginners'* (Kilmarnock, UK: John Ritchie Ltd., 2021) Pgs. 93-107.

what is the 'mark of the beast'?

9 781914 273087 >

Mark Hitchcock says, 'Almost everyone has heard something about the *"666"* also known as 'the mark of the beast". [1]

But exactly what it will be, or how it will work, no one will know. Until the 'Coming Prince' is revealed as the *"Beast"*. He will then have his *"image"* set up in Jerusalem. His *"False Prophet"* will demand global worship. An irreversibly implanted (or branded) 'identifier' will be mandated for all (Rev. 13:16-18). **Only then will it be fully known what the 'mark of the beast' really is!**

what the mark is not

The 'mark of the beast' is not just a barcode, even if it did seem like it - at the time of first using - back in 1974 (patented in the U.S.A. in 1952).

Neither did the *"mark"* follow when the first functioning 'chip' was surgically implanted in a human body, in the U.K. in 1998. [2]

The 'mark' is not just an 'R.F.I.D. chip', even if technology has moved on to such chips being active, able to transmit data from (and about) the user. Able to be sent to an external – and centralised – collector of information.

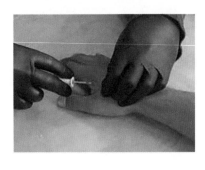

Though devices such as a functioning 'Neuralink Chip' (linked to the human brain) may be realised soon, it does not give licence – for even Bible believers – to cry, 'This is the mark of the beast!' every time science crosses a new neurological, biological, or scientific boundary.

can the 'mark' be received by accident?

The *"mark"* is not a vaccine, or a drug. Nor anything that would allow it to be received accidentally. Scripture is totally clear on this point. Even in the day of God's judgment [which we have looked at] there will still be warnings given about the consequences of rebellion against God. And of 'taking sides' with the forces of Satan.

Scripture makes totally clear the context of when, where, and who the 'mark of the beast' relates to. No mistake will be possible. In that day.

God will use angels, as well as men, to proclaim not only an *"eternal gospel … to those who dwell on earth"* (Rev. 14:6), but also send a final warning, *"If anyone worships the beast and its image and receives a mark on his forehead or on his hand, he also will drink the wine of God's wrath"* (Rev. 14:9-10). This is 'apocalyptic' language suited to the last days, and a divine warning before final judgment. Actions do have consequences, as we have already seen. This will be a deliberate choice. **It will also be irreversible!**

what the mark is

The 'mark of the beast' is not strictly a biblical title. It is rather a 'shorthand' of various titles combined. There are four differing items which John was told of in his Revelation visions regarding the *"beast"* and his *"mark"*:

1. **The Image** (Mat. 24:15; Rev. 13:14). This will be set up in the Temple court in Jerusalem – at the midpoint of the 7 years – to mark the death and 'reappearance' of the man who is called the *"Antichrist"*.
2. **The Mark** (Rev. 13:16). Received on the forehead or right hand by all who want to be identified with, and to worship, the *"Beast"*.
3. **The Name** (Rev. 13:17). This man throughout prophecy has many names. He will appear as a *"Prince"* (Dan. 9:26), but he is essentially evil and a tool of Satan his master.
4. **The Number** (Rev. 13:17-18). Whether the *"666"* will confirm his name, or whatever it represents, it will link all who take it, not only to the *"Beast"*, but also to his Divine destruction (Rev. 14:10). [3]

[1] Hitchcock, M. *'101 Answers About the End Times'* (New York, NY: Multnomah, 2001) Pg. 142.
[2] Warwick, K. Professor of Cybernetics, Reading University, UK. 24th Aug. 1998.
[3] McKillen, M. D. *'End Times for Beginners'* (Kilmarnock, UK: John Ritchie Ltd., 2021) Pgs. 154-156.

is 'Armageddon' a battle?

The 'Plain of Megiddo' looking northwards from the original 'Megiddo Citadel'

Not really. But firstly: Where is *"Megiddo"*? What happened there in the past? Do events from the past give clues as to events in the future?

E.H. Cline an archaeologist excavating in the Valley of Megiddo found evidence of at least 34 battles in the past, 12 of which he said occurred in Bible times. Dr. Israel Finkelstein, from Tel Aviv University and working with Cline, said, 'We are at Megiddo, not only because of … the archaeology, but because of Armageddon' [1]. The past throws light on what is still to come.

Megiddo is a place. A double valley stretching from Haifa, on the Israeli coast, to Beit'Shan on the Golan Heights in the east (more than 60km). It has also been called in Bible times the *"Valley of Jezreel"* (Jud. 6:33). It is known today as 'The Vale of Esdraelon'. Presently mostly arable land.

Megiddo has a past. *"Megiddo"* is mentioned 12 times in O.T. Bible history as a place of war. Joshua had one of his early conquests there, when the *"Children of Israel"* defeated the king of Megiddo (Jos. 12:21). King Josiah of Judah was killed there by *"Pharaoh Necoh"* king of Egypt (2Kin. 23:29-30). In secular history, Napoléon Bonaparte (1769-1821) said, 'Megiddo is the greatest natural battle-site in all of the Middle East'. [2]

Megiddo has a future. The mention of *"Armageddon"* in the book of Revelation (Rev. 16:16) – which translates as 'the mountains of Megiddo' – is the 13th mention in the Bible. A number connected with rebellion. It is God who will *"assemble them for battle"* (Rev. 16:14). The armies of the east, the north, and the south – coming in rebellion against the *"Prince"* – and the armies of the west, probably still loyal to him. Satan will think that he is in control. His plan, regardless of who wins the battle, will be the destruction of Israel and Jerusalem (not a new theme for the devil).

what will happen at Armageddon?

Certainly not a nuclear war. Nor a catastrophe that wipes out the population of earth: Events which the media associate with 'Armageddon'.

1. **Not all the armies will be there.** Some will be in the Moab hills. Some will be south of Jerusalem. Some will probably be northwards, from Syria up. But all will be fully defeated (Isa. 63:1-3).

2. **The armies will not fight each other.** They will combine – at the very last – to fight a common foe. Old adversaries will be forgotten in the face of an unforeseen enemy.

3. **The threat will be new.** And appear suddenly. Every direction is covered (as the Mediterranean Sea is on the west), but this threat will be from the sky. They will see *"in heaven the sign of the Son of Man"* (Mat. 24:30). They will attempt to fight with *"Jehovah's Anointed"*, who is Jesus Christ (Psa. 2:2). But they cannot win!

4. **The *"armies of heaven"* will appear.** Jesus will return as *"King of kings"* (Rev. 19:14,16). The *"Beast"* and the *"False Prophet"* will be captured, and sent alive to *"the lake of fire"* (Rev. 19:20) [Pg. 55].

5. **Every army – every enemy – will be defeated.** None will be left alive. Satan will be defeated as well. **Jesus will return. Again!**

[1] Cline, E. H. & Finkelstein, I. Dr., www.nytimes.com (New York, NY: Jan. 2000)
[2] McKillen, M. D. 'End Times for Beginners' (Kilmarnock, UK: John Ritchie Ltd., 2021) Pgs. 204-206.

is Jesus really coming **back**?

Who is coming?

The question is not, 'Is Jesus coming?' But 'Is it the Jesus of the gospels?' **The Jesus who has been before?** A great many who believe in *"Jesus from Nazareth"* as a figure of 1ˢᵗ Century history do not believe in His <u>deity</u>. Nor in His <u>resurrection</u>. And accordingly, not in His <u>second</u> coming. Yet the biblical record is clear, *"This Jesus, who was taken up from you into heaven, will come in the same way as you saw Him go into heaven"* (Act. 1:11). As He went up, so He will come back. **Jesus Christ has two comings!**

how will He come?

Mark Hitchcock sets out 7 significant characteristics of Jesus' return: He is coming **personally:** *"I am coming quickly"* (Rev. 22:20 NASB). He is coming **literally:** *"I will come again"* (Joh. 14:3). He is coming **visibly:** *"Behold, He is coming … every eye will see Him"* (Rev. 1:7). Every believer – and every enemy – will see the returning Jesus the Messiah. He is coming **suddenly:** *"I will*

come like a thief" (Rev. 3:3). He is coming **dramatically:** *"The Son of Man coming in clouds with great power"* (Mar. 13:26). He is coming **gloriously:** *"with power and great glory"* (Mat. 24:30). He is coming **triumphantly:** *"He has a name … King of kings and Lord of lords"* (Rev. 19:16). **[1]**

Plaque at 'garden tomb' in Jerusalem

where will Jesus come to?

We saw that He will destroy the armies in Moab first (Isa. 63:1), in the Jordanian plains. Then He will *"stand on the Mount of Olives"* and divide the mountain (Zec. 14:4). He will liberate Jerusalem, and then destroy the *"Megiddo"* armies in the north [Pgs.48-49].

what will Jesus come to do?

He will come to defeat His enemies. To regather faithful Israel: *"when I pour out My Spirit upon the house of Israel"* (Eze. 39:29). To judge the living: *"Depart from Me, you cursed"* (Mat. 25:41). To resurrect the O.T.

believers (Dan. 12:1-4). To imprison Satan and bind him, *"for a thousand years"* (Rev. 20:2). To set up His kingdom: *"the God of heaven will set up a kingdom that shall never be destroyed"* (Dan. 2:44).

why is a kingdom on earth necessary?

Even some Christians ask this. Surely the *"Kingdom"* is in heaven? No! There will be a 'heavenly' kingdom forever. And a new earth too. **But many of the wrongs of our world must be put right by Jesus in His coming earthly Kingdom**. Down here! Creation itself must be redeemed (Rom. 8:22-23). The conditions of *"Eden"* will be restored. The O.T. *"covenant"* promises – to Abraham, to David, and through Jeremiah – must have a literal fulfilment: *"I will make of you a great nation"* (Gen. 12:1-3), *"To your offspring I give this land"* (Gen. 15:18). And to David, *"the throne of his kingdom forever"* (2Sam. 7:13). **[2]**

There are over 1,500 prophecies in the O.T. still to be fulfilled. The '1,000 year kingdom' (or *'Millennium'* from Latin) will also fulfil over 300 N.T. promises. **Jesus said He would come back.** Though He is coming for His *"Church"* [the *'Rapture'*, Pgs. 34-35], He must also appear literally, *"the appearing of the glory of our great God and Saviour Jesus Christ"* (Tit. 2:13).

why is the kingdom not 'forever'?

God will show that – even in perfect climatic and environmental conditions – with a perfect government, the heart of mankind is still rebellious. Satan will be released, after the 1,000 years, for one last confrontation:

which he cannot win!

[1] Hitchcock, M. *'101 Answers About the End Times'* (New York, NY: Multnomah, 2001) Pgs. 202-205.
[2] McKillen, M. D. *'End Times for Beginners'* (Kilmarnock, UK: John Ritchie Ltd., 2021) Pgs. 226-237.

is there a **last judgment**?

Yes! The 'Millennial kingdom' is the final proof that only salvation through faith in the death of Jesus Christ is sufficient to make us fit for God's presence: *"For by grace you have been saved through faith. And this is not of your own doing; it is the gift of God, not a result of works, so that no one may boast"* (Eph. 2:8-9). **Anti-social behaviour is often blamed on the environment in which a person grew up. The Scriptures disagree.** Jesus said, *"What comes out of a person is what defiles him … All these evil thoughts come from within, and they defile a person"* (Mar. 7:20-23).

At the end of the 'Kingdom Age' Satan will be released, and will find millions to gather to him in a final rebellion! Henry Morris wrote, 'After 1,000 years of a perfect environment, with … no external temptation to sin … there is still a multitude of unsaved … who are ready to rebel against the Lord'. [1]

This army will march on Israel and Jerusalem (for the very last time), but fire will come down and consume them. And the devil *"who had deceived them was thrown into the lake of fire … where the beast and the false prophet (are), and they will be tormented day and night forever and ever"* (Rev. 20:10). Those two evil men will have been there for 1,000 years. Their master Satan will join them. Forever.

there is no annihilation?

No! The Bible does not ever teach the 'annihilation of the soul'. Mark Hitchcock says, 'The Greek word ('*aionios*') which is translated *"eternal"* or *"everlasting"* is used 71 times in the N.T. … It is used of the happiness of the saved in heaven … it is used twice of the duration of God in His glory (Rom. 16:26) … Seven times it is used of the fate of the wicked … without end (Mat. 18:8)'. [2]

'The happiness of heaven for everyone', or 'No afterlife at all' are not biblical concepts. No matter how comforting the ideas may be to many!

Interestingly, despite increasing atheistic dogma in the 20th and 21st centuries, the general belief in the 'afterlife' has not lessened. [3]

what about hell?

After the last earthly rebellion is over and all the rebels are dead ...

What then? John – in his vision – said, *"I saw the dead, great and small, standing before the throne, and books were opened ... And the sea gave up the dead who were in it, Death and Hades gave up the dead who were in them, and they were judged, each one of them, according to what they had done"* (Rev. 20:12-13). All the 'unbelieving' dead will rise again.

The destination of all *"unbelieving"* – from every age – will be the *"great white throne"* of Jesus' final judgment (Rev. 20:11). **Why should anyone be there?** There is no need! None are 'pre-destined' to be there. We can have forgiveness through the death of Jesus. John also wrote, *"Him who loves us and has freed us from our sins by His blood ... to Him be glory ... forever"* (Rev. 1:5-6).   **Forgiveness is here. And now. But not then.**

the lake of fire forever?

Judgment will be from the record of the books which will be open. The *"book of works"* – for sin unforgiven. The Word of God – to show that all are without excuse.

The *"book of life"* – to show whose names are missing from its pages, *"And if anyone's name was not found written in the book of life, he was thrown into the lake of fire"* (Rev. 20:15). [4]   **A final destiny. Forever.**

[1] Morris, H. M. *'The Revelation Record'* (Wheaton, IL: Tyndale House, 1983) Pgs. 419-420.
[2] Hitchcock, M. *'101 Answers About the End Times'* (New York, NY: Multnomah, 2001) Pgs. 235-236.
[3] CBS News Poll. (Roper Centre, New York, NY: 2014) ropercenter.cornell.edu
[4] McKillen, M. D. *'End Times for Beginners'* (Kilmarnock, UK: John Ritchie Ltd., 2021) Pgs. 243-244.

where are you going?

A great many of the questions in this booklet have been taken from those which have been asked – by others – to people who are believers in Jesus Christ. One of the great fundamental questions is: '**Why are we hopeful about the future?**' Our response, based on the Word of God is, 'Because of what the gospel message of 'salvation by faith alone' tells us'.

Three great pillars of the gospel are:

1. Jesus died for sinners *"Christ died for our sins in accordance with the scriptures"* (1Cor. 15:3).

2. Jesus rose again *"He was buried … He was raised on the third day according to the scriptures"* (1Cor. 15:4).

3. Jesus will return to reign *"He must reign until He has put all His enemies under His feet"* (1Cor. 15:25).

These cannot be separated, or the very *"hope"* – certainty – of Christianity will collapse, as a building founded on sand.

You must agree that if 'all of the above' are true; then **Jesus Christ was, and is, the Son of God. And that therefore He can be your Saviour.**

Not just for the 'here and now' but for the 'forever'. For time and eternity. Lee Strobel wrote, 'If my conclusion in 'The Case for Christ' is correct, your future and eternity hinge on how you respond to Christ. As Jesus Himself declared, *"Unless you believe that I am He you will die in your sins"* (Joh. 8:24)'. [1]

Christians believe that, just as Jesus went away, so He will suddenly return (Act. 1:11). We will be safe in heaven for a short time when the *"wrath to come"* is happening on earth (1The. 1:10). Then we will share His Kingdom, with Him, for 1,000 years on this earth.

what happens after that?

We have already seen that the *"kingdom"* is not the end [Pgs. 52-53]. After the 1,000 years are ended. After Satan is released. After the last judgment, after the *"great white throne"* (Rev. 20:11) … **What then?**
There will be a *"new heaven and a new earth"* (Rev. 21:1). There will be a *"holy city, new Jerusalem"* (Rev. 21:2). Jesus Himself said to John, *"Behold, I am making all things new."* (Rev. 21:5). The servants of God will worship Him, *"and they will reign forever and ever"* (Rev. 22:5). Happy forever!

What about you? Perhaps when you started reading this booklet you had a very different mindset? Perhaps you still do. Or perhaps your thinking has altered a little about the claims of Christianity and its central figure, Jesus Christ? Perhaps you are ready to acknowledge the claims of the Bible, that Jesus can be your Saviour from your sins [Pgs. 28-29]. And from their penalty [Pgs. 54-55; 60-61]: **The choice is yours!**

As is the choice regarding your destiny. For your spirit and soul will live forever, and God will decree – **according to your choice in your lifetime** – which destiny will be yours. Forever. There is no changing of sides on the other side. There is *"eternal destruction"* (2The. 1:9) for all unbelievers, and an *"everlasting kingdom"* (Psa. 145:13) for the saved. 'What a hope to gladden the heart of every believer … a kingdom of eternal peace and purity, with Jesus Christ as King forever' [2]. **There is hope now!**

[1] Strobel, L. *'The Case for Christ'* (Grand Rapids, MI: Zondervan, 2016) Pg. 293.
[2] McKillen, M. D. *'End Times for Beginners'* (Kilmarnock, UK: John Ritchie Ltd., 2021) Pgs. 307-308.

simple chronology of **Bible times:**

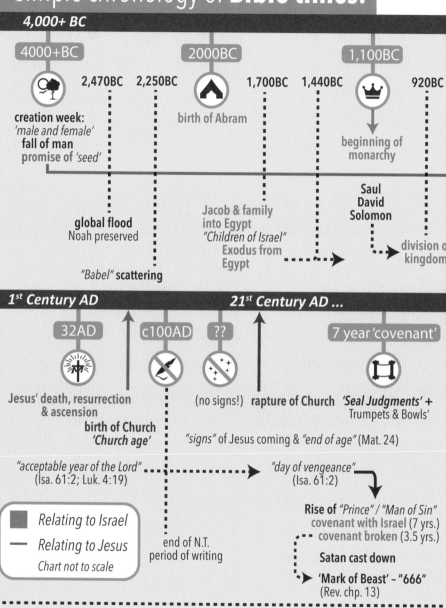

4,000+ BC

4000+BC   2,470BC   2,250BC   **2000BC**   1,700BC   1,440BC   **1,100BC**   920BC

creation week:
'male and female'
fall of man
promise of *'seed'*

birth of Abram

beginning of monarchy

global flood
Noah preserved

**Saul
David
Solomon**

"Babel" **scattering**

Jacob & family
into Egypt
"Children of Israel"
Exodus from
Egypt

**division of
kingdom**

1ˢᵗ Century AD   21ˢᵗ Century AD ...

32AD   **c100AD**   **??**   **7 year 'covenant'**

**Jesus' death, resurrection
& ascension**

(no signs!) **rapture of Church**

'Seal Judgments' +
Trumpets & Bowls'

**birth of Church
'Church age'**

"signs" of Jesus coming & *"end of age"* (Mat. 24)

"acceptable year of the Lord"
(Isa. 61:2; Luk. 4:19)

"day of vengeance"
(Isa. 61:2)

Rise of *"Prince" / "Man of Sin"*
covenant with Israel (7 yrs.)
covenant broken (3.5 yrs.)

■	*Relating to Israel*
—	*Relating to Jesus*
	Chart not to scale

end of N.T.
period of writing

Satan cast down

'Mark of Beast' – "666"
(Rev. chp. 13)

N.T. period (cont.)

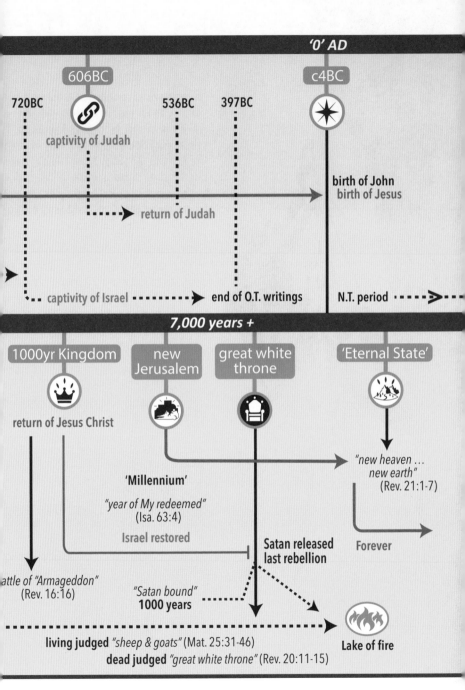

Have you ever counted how many times you use the word 'hope' from when you wake up in the morning? If you do, it might surprise you how much of your life is lived 'hoping'. From trivial issues like hoping there is milk in the fridge to the more serious 'hoping' there will be no more Covid or stabbings on our streets - the list is endless.

One reason we 'hope' is that we know there are so many variables in life that can alter the outcome of circumstances. True hope therefore must offer unchangeable unmoveable security all day every day. But does such a thing exist in our ever-changing world not to mention the virtual world?

Only a true Christian can say with certainty that true hope really does exist, and not only in this world but the next. This booklet has been written to show that the only person in whom we can find true hope is God. One of His titles is *"the God of hope"* (Rom. 15:13).

We can hope in God because His Word is true and reliable. The Bible is 'God-breathed' and tells us it is impossible for God to lie. Secondly, we can hope in God because He is able to reveal our faults yet knows exactly how to make us right. We may not like to admit our faults but that is like a person going to the doctor and because they dislike the diagnosis they ignore the cure - fatal!

But some argue, 'I don't commit all the sins some people do and therefore don't deserve

hope?

...or are you just hoping for the best?

God's wrath'. But that is also fatal thinking because it measures how good you are by other people and not God. God said, *"None is righteous"* (Rom. 3:10).

Imagine you were a rock climber dangling over a cliff by a chain and all the links of the chain snapped. What would happen? You would fall to your death. But if just one link snapped what is the outcome? Exactly the same, and so it is with God's law. If we break one link it's all broken, and we fall under the same death sentence of a Holy and just God,

"And just as it is appointed for man to die once, and after that comes judgment" (Heb. 9:27).

"For there is no distinction: for all have sinned and fall short of the glory of God" (Rom. 3:22-23). It is hopeless trying to impress God with our good works.

The fault that causes all humanity to sin is traced back to the first man Adam who ignored God's instructions and did things his own way. His wilful disobedience brings the whole world under God's legal verdict: *"guilty"* (Rom. 3:19).

The good news is that God's plan of salvation offers eternal hope in a man with no faults. His name is Jesus Christ and in Him there is no sin. **It was impossible for Jesus Christ to sin and as the sinless Son of God He alone was qualified to die for our sins on the cross.** There He paid for eternal life for us even though our sins deserved eternal death in hell. God is willing to give us the gift of eternal life if we repent from our sins and trust in Jesus Christ as our personal Saviour. God will wipe the slate clean so that we are forgiven, cleansed, fit for Heaven and saved from the wrath to come. But this hope God offers is more than a place in Heaven...

God says the hope of eternal life is an *"anchor of the soul"* (Heb. 6:19). - an anchor in the waves of death but also on the great sea of life in every circumstance we face. If we are saved then every day we can be sure the God of hope is with us and His Word will be our navigation. It doesn't promise that life will be without storms or injury but it does mean when the wind of feelings and circumstances change we have a Saviour, Jesus Christ who is *"the same yesterday, and today, and for ever"* (Heb. 13:8). The anchor is fixed in Heaven attached to a risen living hope. A dead man offers no hope but Jesus is not dead. He said, *"I am alive forevermore"* (Rev. 1:18).

You might hope you pass your exams this year but if not you can always do them again. With end of life decisions, however, you only have one opportunity. It is no use 'hoping for the best.' Jim Elliot a famous missionary said, *'When it comes time to die, make sure that all you have to do is die.'*

"Believe in the Lord Jesus Christ and you will be saved" (Acts 16:31).

There is no other hope!

[JB]

what comes **next**?

a change of mind?

Jesus came *"proclaiming the gospel of God, and saying, 'The time is fulfilled, and the kingdom of God is at hand; <u>repent</u> and <u>believe</u> in the gospel"* (Mar. 1:14-15).

[underlined by author]

What does 'repentance' mean? It means even more than a change of mind: A reversal of my 'purpose and decision'. A 180° turn around in my thoughts – perhaps about God – certainly about myself …

Not 'doing' or 'paying' [Pgs. 24-25] or even 'baptism'. Being *"baptized"* as a believer in Jesus Christ is very good, and is required (Act. 8:36-38). But only after conversion **[1]**. The ritual of 'infant baptism' does nothing at all, and even as an adult a 'baptism' ceremony cannot save!

Paul said he was, *"testifying both to Jews and to Greeks* (Gentiles) *of repentance toward God and of faith in our Lord Jesus Christ"* (Act. 20:21).

Those are the key elements to salvation: 'Repentance' and 'faith' in Jesus.

[1] Hay, J. *'Baptism'* (Kilmarnock, UK: John Ritchie Ltd., 2010) Pg. 12.

Have you other questions you would like answered?

Has the booklet helped you to answer any of your questions?

Please contact the author at: whatintheworldishappening@gmail.com

OR

www.neverthirstagain.co.uk

If you would like a copy of a New Testament (state language preference)

Please contact the author, or the Publisher at:

John Ritchie Ltd. 40 Beansburn, Kilmarnock, Scotland, KA3 1RL

If you need further help, please contact the following:

would you like to know more about coming events?

An overview of all biblical prophecy is available by the same author:

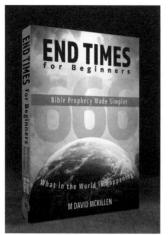

'In this clearly written and fully illustrated book, David has provided us with an enjoyable and accurate outline of Bible prophecy. This study is not only ideal for beginners, but will be helpful for older Christians who feel the need to revisit these important truths. Highly recommended.'

John F. Parkinson
(Author of 'No Other Doctrine - The Gospel and the Postmodern World')

ISBN: 978 1 914273 08 7
John Ritchie Ltd., UK. (Dec. 2021)
www.ritchiechristianmedia.co.uk

350 pages, full colour, fully illustrated and with index and appendices included

---

about the author:

David McKillen was born and raised in Northern Ireland. He came to faith in Jesus Christ as his personal Saviour in 1967. After a career in retail and marketing, he left secular employment in 2004, and with his wife Helen went into full-time mission work, firstly in southern Africa and then further afield.

He has had a life-long interest in current affairs, and geo-political events, as seen from a biblical worldview. This interest, combined with public Bible teaching, and a recent on-line ministry (since the commencement of Covid in 2020), led to the beginning of his written ministry.

'Essential Questions for End Times' is his most recent publication (July 2022).